AXIS Z BOOK 3
AJ CARRUTHERS

Other publications by a j carruthers

AXIS Book 1: 'Areal'
AXIS Book 2
Consonata
EPSON L4168 consonant studies
Literary History and Avant-Garde Poetics in the Antipodes:
   Languages of Invention
MS Word Variations 1-11
Stave Sightings: Notational Experiments in North American
   Long Poems
The Blazar Axes

AXIS

Z BOOK 3

A J CARRUTHERS

BOOK 07
SERIES 5

CORDITE
BOOKS

First printed in 2023
by Cordite Publishing Inc.

PO Box 393
Carlton South 3053
Victoria, Australia
cordite.org.au | corditebooks.org.au

National Library of Australia
Cataloguing-in-Publication:

  Carruthers, A J
  Axis Z Book 3
  978-0-6457616-0-3 paperback
  I. Title.
  A821.3

Public Domain images on cover: Katsushika Hokusai's samurai,
Album of Sketches (1760–1849), Skull and a Rib Cage (c.1800–1900),
Sangi Takamura (c.1800–1900); William Hogarth's Characters and
Caricatures: subscription ticket for 'Marriage à la Mode' (1743);
William Blake 'Job Rebuked by His Friends' (1825).

Poetry set in Rabenau 10 / 15 by a j carruthers
Cover design by Zoë Sadokierski
Series text design by Kent MacCarter and Zoë Sadokierski
Printed and bound by McPherson's Printing Group
Maryborough, Victoria

10 9 8 7 6 5 4 3 2 1

CONTENTS

PREFACE

Dear Readers: I hope you have a good experience reading this book. *Z Book* 3 is the third of my long poem *AXIS*, coming nearly one decade after the first. The first two, *AXIS Book 1: 'Areal'* and *AXIS Book 2*, were both written in 'vertical stanzas'. These prioritised not left to right but top to bottom running of words, as with various calligraphic traditions. Writing downward in columns allows for very long lines. *AXIS Z Book 3* is no different in that regard.

No special skill is required for reading this book. The 'structure', if one should call it that, of the phrasing is mostly a 'Let ... For' syntax, which was used by Christopher Smart in *Jubilate Agno* (1759–1763). Smart does praise and prophecy. *Z Book 3* is more praise than prophecy. Voices not my own came from innumerable places and times to speak in the Mythic System of *Z Book* 3 – characters both major and minor, they speak at will.

It was written in the midst of a grave imbalance among the axes of the world, which produces war. I dedicate *Z Book 3* to the Peace Forces of this Earth, and to a greater material and spiritual share between nations.

INTRODUCTION

In a j carruthers's new collection, verse stanzas, running vertically from top to bottom rather than left to right, challenge the dominant linear mode of thinking and writing in the West. They call attention to alternative forms of representation and reveal the existence of other landscapes. The purpose of the 'axis' is no longer confined to one-way movement, but to rotation and circular modes of thinking, writing, and generating new ideas.

The poems here are iconoclastic: they draw on different media (such as musical notation) and languages, and avoid standard lyrical and stylistic forms. They can be read non-sequentially, and in open-ended ways that invite the reader's participation. The poet's defamiliarising techniques create a certain degree of difficulty and slow the progress of perception. Reading in this case is never easy or smooth, but an exercise in aesthetic entertainment and critical thinking.

carruthers's poems also remind me of the palindromic poems in the Chinese poetic tradition, especially those by Su Hui, in pre–Qin Dynasty China. Su Hui wove a 'reversible circular-picture poem' for her husband Dou Tao, who had been exiled to the place of 'flowing sands'. This mournful poem of love's longing consists of 840 characters and can be read horizontally, vertically, backwards, forwards – in any direction – to make over 200 other poems, and won the admiration of the Empress Wu Zetian.

AXIS Z Book 3 displays an alter–avant-garde modernism: the poems continue, on the one hand, the tradition of modernism (recalling something of e. e. cummings or Ezra Pound); and, on the other, the heritage of marginal writers and writings neglected in Eurocentric modernist studies. This is more than a game of words:

the poems are, the poet states, 'written in an environment of a great imbalance of worlds, which produces war'. Just as the poetry of Su Hui bears her love for her husband, *AXIS Z Book* 3 bears the empathy of this poet for the world, while also bearing witness to the limits of language in the face of human progress.

—Wang Guanglin

Z-book
Book of Praise

ZERO

Let
Liboteur
do
th
work
of
Prophet
who
is
NOT
ACCEPTED
YET.

Let
Huitzilopochti
Gerzil
Rongo
Set
Hachiman
Inanna almighty
Indra
Junda
Jiutian Xuannü
Nemain
Laran
&
th
Kydoimos
Neit
Idis
Ullr
Jarovit
Sekhmet
&
Ogoun
&
Resheph
&
Enyo
REJOICE
with
Roberto

Let
Nicholas
Pounder
th
PRINTERPRETER (Bk 1)
rejoice
in
th
Spirit
of
his
ways
with
Blake
Hokusai
Hogarth
who
legislate
shape.

Let
Nick
Whittock
&
Cathy
Vidler
VISUALISE
th
Quantum
Universe
&
Wicket
Pitch
SPATIALLY
INTUIT
spontaneously
exercising
caution
O,
o.

th
Clown
who
would
U
believe
VERTICALLY
REGISTERED ZERO
more
on
it
later.

63.   Zero

Let
th
First Zero
attach
itself
to
an
empty
number
&
set
th
PAGE.

Let
th
Second Zero
be
STENCH
&
is
τελευταίος
to
BRONZAIT
th
B
in
lieu
of
WAR DEITIES
Frosterus of
closer:
Be pleased
@
these
solemn &
frenetic
encomia
producing
Zola
power.

Let
th
Third Zero
be
PRAISE
th
Eternal Prognosticator
votive
on
Giuseppe
A.L. Barbauld
who
farms
fairly
collecting
Thought:
suurennuslasi?
th
Prophet
is
no
Messenger
of
Peace,
ok,
Leave
reference
here.

Let
th
Fourth Zero
appear
everywhere
as
telling
us
abouth
Humanities:
these
are
my
meanings,
no
prophetie
here,
no
nothing
eythr.

Let
Saboteur
take
no
advice
from
FRIGHTEN
pursuing
Nurbiy
through
Poinsett County
jkeliáuti
m.

Let
Souers
pay
th
carrossier
arriving
insulem
{Seventeen Ninety-Nine
{Seventeen Seventy
póssessing
nothing
Zenning
becoz
th
State-Owned
Enterprises
are
getting
restless
&
won't
pay
won't
pay
for
TUNING
where
are
we

Let
CD Smart
tell
W. McGonagall
&
R. Southey?
they

need
not
be
WELL-WROUGHTED
praise-
phrase
th
Language
Unadorned
will
B
th In harmony
of
th Theorhoea
MEANING THAT:
Zed
gleaming
has
zeal
now

Let
Sandy gallito
go
terendo
with
Vince
&
th
Carmelites
frankly
look
fetching
as
they
iz.

ah
Entifying
nothing
Restful
art
praise
Arthur
liberalising
I
mean
liberalizing
space
Tito-izm!
TAKEAWAY
EPIC
noticed
of'th
little
bit
Enjoyment
of
Meaning
uh.

now
Zestful
Zapatistas
now
now
EXAMINE
other
Distances
please.

65. Zest

Let
mighty
PROCOPTODON
show
Presbyterians
th
way
to
Hogue
Run.

Let
Shi & Tao
at
great
pido
стационар
encountering
Szentgyörgyi
merkantil
consorting
with
Phillippine
Baptists
going
to
th
Detention
Hospital
to
defeat
TH TOES
&
TH VEHICLES—
which
Age
animates
Era?

Let
Multan
meekwame
Bisping
&
NEOWISE
find
Ascension
in
Venetiola,
&
you
too,
H.S. Herndon,
getting
ENSCONCED
in
Bankend
around
Bedford.

Let
Kyrgyz
over
kivilattia
bear
th
burden
of
that
internoscanmini
reprendes
which
despises
Hiteswar,
Bhut
&
th
opinionated
Wombats.

66. Zayin

Let
B. Pascoe
Thought
produce
crafty
HOURGLASS
PRODUCTIVITY
**(TIME'S
UP
don't
rush)**
Nabonidus
Now
Focus!
Fogman
Fogs
Loudly
Louder
Loudest
Flatulator,
helping
ARCTIC
ADVENTURES
called
off
Sentinel
Sham
on.

Let
A. Couani
(hi)
oversee
mutual
worderers
everywhere
don't
worry
A. Stewart
producing
Seven5
hours
of
Benedictory
Music
musical.ly.

Let
H. Hooton
about
huh?
ah
th Craterites
Subjection
getting
accessible
&
kicking
North
zound
Avant
Garde,
Zayin:
**Polit-
Bureaucracy**
will
make
a
Match
melt.

Let
V. Ah Kee
see
in
Beyköy
masters of
carrying
SELENITE
stones
Sort
of
—
Haller-velu
Fiat-velu
Lidl-velu
Enedine-velu
**on
an
Iseline.**

Zayn

Let
Packet
th
Unknown
John
ride
upon
ACTIVE GALACTIC
Understanding in
Pap-nigin-gara
&
let
OUTSCAPEN
VERS
be
near
an Oxygen
equivalent
of
Vertical
Deflection.

Let
Ohlsdorf
know
th
right
jargon
just
AXIALITIES as
case
Greb
sees
Maria
Amadeus,
Th
Happy:
Grace-
Beauty or
Faith-
Grace Th
DARKLING
BEETLE
raiding
th
Digital
Darkroom.

Let
Nearly
mourn
with
Sportly
contacting
Baanwielrennertjes
th
Present
Science
on
Long
Long Pontiffs
or
Otto Dix
exults`
DIVYENNDU
under
th
Cyprian
Bridge.

Let
BLAZAR
please
Schnittke
as
much
as
Coates
Gorecki,
Franssens,
Oliveros,
Tan
of Lafón
MONTSERRAT,
Tornado-Flying
dropping
Zola
appreciates
Treatises
flat
out
n
on
th
run
EXCEPT
JAK
who

iz
dishonest
&
needs
Arthur
to
write
it
down
for
him!

Let
V. Namatjira
sanctify
Woga
with
th
Pompographica,
naturally
depicting
th
National
Academical
Peace
Highway
Foundation
Trust
playing
CRAB CANON
to
th
King.

Let
Thalia
sanctify
G.M. Hopkins
with
th
Potamidae
&
Nidara
Multiversa
for
th
Universe
whose
Instress'
corresponding
Outstress
sounds
good
be's
gracious
to
Berardi
&
Th Practical
Cactus
&
blessed
th

Let
Steenacker
sanctify
Th Brownings
with
th
Propleopus
th
CARNIVOROUS
KANGAROO
who
feeds
Cottonclad
upon
Ram
upon
Fountainfire
there
being
FIFTEEN
SATELLITE
SERVICES
Ten
to
Th Antipode
none
encrypted
&
speaking

Let
T.V. Topping
sanctify
Esiso
with
th
Oscillans
THUNDERBIRD
Dromornis
Stirtoni
DEMON
DUCK
OF
DOOM
who
enlists
Ampfield
&
restores
Treatia
HINAGDANAN
is
bravely
Pertaining
blessed
be
Arnold
increasing

Bo
Locomotive
you
are
Whole:
Colleran
&
Kominato.

plainly
favouring
Diocese Salads
tossed
for
Minori
Teardrop
Mirambeau
Monte Camicia
&
ODIN-OSIRIS
blessing
th
Centre
for
Discovery.
.

Clara
th
Pudding
who
resides.

69.   Zigzag

Let   Let   Let   Let
Detour   Sukanaivalu,   Blakespear   Ahania
Front   Front   Front   Front
of   of   of   of
Anvil   Sandwich,   New Prague   Middle Kingdom
exult   exult   exult   exult
th   th   th   th
Silky Frankenia Robust Greenhood   Nightcap
per   &   Grass-Fern   Oak
Wagin Banksia; Ninghan Violet exult   **bless**
please   **alongside**   Corunna Daisy Blunt
consecrate   Swamp Starflower   Wattle &
&   neatly.   exult   Hemlock
purify   Triggerplant   woolly
Mingenew Everlasting   screamer,   adelgid
Pearlwort   nurture   quotation
too.   Stiff Groundsel which
                                    who   won't
                                    is   make
                                    a   U
                                    Sensible   laugh.
                                    Plant.

Let
Ζ
imply
Sword
suggesting
disappointingly
large
droopy
Sickles
ȝ
Energia
hiding
TH CONSONANTS
being
SUBSTANCE
&
vowels
ACCIDENTALS
&
th
ɛ
At . . .
AH I SEE
It means
Hammer
Th consonants
Listen:
Poor
Saints

Let
Ζ
signify
dibosons
denoting
th
DELPHI
observations
equate
ȝ
with
Rodrigo,
keeping
distance
unbelievably
laughing
&
th
ɛ
at
last
Entifying
nothing.

Let
Ζ
imply
Ischia
signifies
blame,
blame
of Sacred Consonants
dropping,
ȝ
compare
SEIJO
with
JONG AH SIU, look
th
latter
lesser-
known
&
th
ɛ:
at
what?
Outspeaking
historical
Siug,
&
Sing
ENOUGH NOW

Let
Ζ
signify
Izzard
meaning
Alphabeast
flailing
wailing
ȝ
First
Isthmus-
Nature—
Electronics
r very
not
good
&
th
ɛ
at
Arthur
prophorikos:
revelation
in
guarded
tongue.

stuck

with

A QUOTE ZED:

YOU TASTE TH YOGHURT

YOU TASTE TH YOGHURT

TASTE N TELL

ZAYS MAURICE BISHOP TH BAOIST

PASSES IT ON TO HUA, WHO PASSES IT TO DENG,

TITO, RAUL & TH LITTLE SCOT

IN TH MARKET

IN TH MARKET WITH TH STALLS

NOTHING TO SEE HERE

NOTHING TO ASK

DON'TELL THEM

DON'TELL THEM ABOUT SCHOLAR-CORRUPTER

WT TH RESEARCH PLAN & DUN HISTORY

WE HEARD

WHAT YOU WA ZAYIN.

WORSHIPS TH AMERICANS

TASTE TH YOGHURT

TASTE N TELL

EASY DUN IT RAHMON

EASY DUN IT

CLAMORUS WORLD!

Let	Let	Let	Let
Manic Mechanic	Prohorus	Monkeywrench	T. Campion
&	&	Matthias	sing
Elves	Prochorus	&	songs
exult	exult	Hayduke Ezekiel	to
Ewbank	Suetonius	practice	Sherry
with	who	Arbory	NEEDVILLE
th	hears	instead	upon
Regeneration	MYSTERIOUS	of	Yard
Service	VOICES	Augury	who
rhetoric	mostly	because	in
'rhetoric of'	haunted	Zett	turn
What?	histories	zays:	sings
Mr.	**Reik**	Rochelle	**Excessively**
Maximum	going	encountered	**toward**
Televenezuela	off	Miriam	**th**
Monster;	happy-	of	APPRENTICE
What?	to-	th	LISTENER
over	help	CYMBALS	who
there	prophecy	which	praises
is	but	crash.	Choruses
Ernie	clearly		by
Gehr	(Darogan)		nite
FLABBERGASTED			☺.
becoz?	becoz		
	th		
	Posthumous State		
	was		
	th		

experience
of
going
ON & ON
&
of
BEGINNING AGAIN & AGAIN
THIS WAS
ZETT
Please,
an easy read an
acclamation
befitting
U.

72.　Zee

Let Deadhandle handle Ikumi near Chambéry-Sud + meet **George, Dennis Grady** & flee hormonelike from Trident.

Let Jackson of th LIGHT exult in J. Retallack's Reasonable Beatitudes **FIVE** Gnostics. Regarding TH UNKNOWN LETTER... why do Fugues when U can do a Z.

LET JOHN CHRYSOSTOM tell us about th GENDERS rejoicing with th **Hurufiyya** being little bit frightened overall.

Let Pam Brown & Javant Biarujia speak Etruscan with Momodou arrempujar together at **a time** convenient to all.

Zither

Let
Advanced
Imaging
be
of
use
to
BOWERWOMAN
&
BOWERWOMAN
усыпем
&
Shavazi
of
Cortes
Generales
&
jalásemos
ground
to
th
ground
&c.

Let
there
be
something
happening
somewhere
that
isn't
going
to
handle
Thickly +
trickily
th
Queens of Europe
&
all
th
Tiny Green Owls
Stiria satana
standing
by
producin'
praise
Determining:
th
height

Let
Mikuno
rejoice
with
Rajasa
whose
felientem
meets
стандартна
speaking
Ledo Kaili
to
th
Desert
Fathers
tell
us
again
in
th
corner
of
an
uninhabited
cell.

Let
Character
&
Genre
wither
th FRATRES
whether
or
not
PERSONAGES
like Philtre
producin
Zither
&
composin
rly
listen
&
pray.

of
th
Participant
th
motive
of
th
DISSENTING
CITIZEN,
th
type
of
GOVERNMENT-CITIZEN
CONCERNED,
AN
TH
HAPPY
LITTLE
GOVERNMENT
ITSELF.

Let	Let	Let	Let
C. Wolff	I. Burn	H. Darboven	T. Hsieh
set	assay	disturb	hear
M. Tighe	Burn's	th	th
to	SONGS	remains	voice
Music	while	of	of
outscaping	demonstrating	F. Hemans	Takehito Koyasu
DARK	Pharoah's	finding	playing
DISHARMONYS		Roberto	Nosutoradamusu
OF	SHEETS OF SOUND		u
TH	**possessing**	Stealing	know
SPHERES	**nothing**	Opus	th
hang	on	given	SHAPE
on	an	that	of
a	old	SILBERMANN	th
minute	upright.	ORGANS	CONSONANT
isn't		**also**	affected
it		**r powered**	by
making		**by**	Accident
CLALENDARS		**Zola.**	of
fantastic			VOWEL
Clalendars			given
is			molossus?
Like			ye
Two-hundred fifty-sixth notes			that
going on			one.
Simultaneously?			

Let
Ahania
fear
to
associate
with
CARRUTHERSCHOLARLY
CARRUTHERSZenith
from
Crothers
from
Th Bruce
Li Macau
Guangdong Province
Hong Kong
somewhere
CARRUTHERSoul
issue
forth
your
achievements
in
an
abashed
Tone
expected
Now:
WRATH upon Andy
CARRUTHERSNor

Let
Enion
enter
MODERN-
OBLIVION
capping
SCHOLARLY attention
Zenith **of**
since:
being
Practical
Exterior
shell
of
th
&
th
Gyres
glinter
rose
got
from
Maimonides
an
others

Let
Vala
happily
prevaricate
enjoying
th
Liberal Democracy
but
at
Stanley
Stanley
of
th
VOLVOS
here's
th
Deal:
lined
up
in
Good
Order
I
zed
Andy
doesn't
put

Let
Enitharmon
calm
th scope
th scope
praise
th
obskur
Carruthers
prosidys
of
Book 2
brash
predicting
nothing-
,
Now,
zay
what Deal?
m.
WRATH upon
th
Practical
Cactus
that'll
speak
to
th
Greek

praised	is	WRATH upon	
liberally	he	speech	**Mastiff**
Hildegarde	frightened	pulling	**in**
inward	WRATH uponout		**Molossi.**
&	th	th	
downward.	unbroken	techniques	
	line	composed	
	O,	in	
	o,	air.	

Words **composed out of dust**
putting th ink in
Benediction **in** th ink
there is something in th ink
wiped off
meaning vitriol
They think you can **wipe off**
th vitriol
Benediction in th ink
put **out of dust**
in th ink.

76.   Zenith

Let
U.S.aint
Gloria
Coates
who
realises
beholding
in
Liza Lim
**DIABOLICAL
BIRDS**
Betty-
epitomy . . . . .
iz
stressing
SYMPHONIC
WORDS
freely
without
commas—
Hildegarde VB
zays hi
In th
expanded
present.

Let
U.S.aint
Pauline
Oliveros
who
exteriorises,
behold
now
th
DIVINE
CISTERN
tuned
priori
**To
th Greatest**
SOCIALISM
Interior
composing
like
Composers
composing
musical
marginalia.

Let
U.S.aint
Alison
Knowles
who
surely
acknowledges
BEAN
FACULTY
becos
this
is
a
Bk,
Praise
&
explain
Zeniths
as
a
Z-title
so it therefor goes
A-Z
Z-A–U.S.A.
are
you
reading?

Let
U.S.aint
Annea
Lockwood
who
ransacks
Opuses
Now,
becos
th
Zenith
of
Lockwood
is
WOODEN-
PIANO,
fly
flying
woodbits,
nonchalantly,
yes
really.

YEARBOOK

Let
Ruatara Chief
rejoice
with
BEATRICE
Anti-prophet.

'For
Z
is
zest'
(Smart)
&
zest
(Patesion Saga)
iz
ranting
TH SCOPE
FIERY
TH
SCOPE
Zest
ABIEZER HINT
speeches
of
th
concinnity
of
th juncture

Let
Apocalypse
Child
in
arktiskākie
value
Siqueira
silhouettes.

For
Eternal
Infinite
Absolute
&

have
been
ADEQUATELY
DIFFERENTIATED
DISENCUMBRED
BY
th
Philosophers.
Now,
in
my
voice
Rochelle,

Let
Purchase
release
Anxiousness
&
innumerable
literary
references.

FOR
JEFFREY
UPON
LAQALEH
LAQALEH glorifies
Ineffable   th
Liboteurs
J.U.L. HANG ON
WORSHIPS
AN
THOSE
BIBLIOTICIANS
Kohutians
Graphoanalysts
Vaccinologists
taken upon *Siginoth*
& bringed . . .
to th very consinnity
in speech fluidly

& of	Rochelle,	speaking
Th prosimetric kept	out
Number.	calm.	like: fluke.
Ob.	Ob.	Ob.
of prosaic metre		prosaic harmoniesainted
that	explaining	prosaic dissonant
is	However,	prosaic jigg
in	unfortunately	SPEKE! BEETLES
us	mistaken	BEETLES ON TH TRAK
but	just	get
Antipodal.	**means:**	off!
Sol.	**Sol.**	Sol.
rhetor	**rhetor**	rhetor
antiphonal	conditionally	academic
th	decides	**which**
State-Owned	that	**isn't**
Enterprises	Roberto,	**enjoyable**
are	inwardly	speaking
seething	dying,	out
at	zed	speaking
stoppable	'	JAK TH TRUANT
Heat.	Please	OLD FAKE.
	Cover	
	bottom	
	lid.	

78.   Year of the Sorrowful Songs

Let
Collected
lets
authorize
Courteousness
&
legitimise
Unconsciousness
For
Dust
is
not
dross
&
th
Scrolls
&
ICEBLOCK
neither
Epic
nor
Prophetic.

Let
Criticism
by
which
LIT criticism
fallows
ald
meaning
Axis,
mean:
Energy
READING REVIVAL INK WISH
n rereading.

For
my
VISIONS
PRESAGES
mántis
PROGNOSTICATIONS
will
appease
&
displease
my
friends
PIERCING
as
of

Let
Copyright
determine
how
long
VERTICAL VERSE
narratives
striven so
striven so
Meaning ugliness,
spiral out

norigin.

For
ICE
is
shap'd
accordingly
&
th
Galaxy
Cluster
that
is
HELL
goin
up

unceasing	&
noise	**up**
SORROWFUL**to**	
SONGS	**th flank**
alongside	**Others out there** ...
this	*th*
be	Other
read	down
STANZA ROTUNDA	
really why.	th
	eye
	of
	th
	Double Hypercane —

Ob.
yes
Talmud
personal
Impersonal.

Ob.
no
no
yes
Intuition.

Ob.
no
no
no
GYR in th mud . . . . .

Sol.
A
language
everybody can
Hmm.

Sol.
Now,
in
understand
th
expanded
present
WARNING ABOUT AUSTALGIA
LURK IN TH SHADOWS
CARRYING ZYMBOLS
ZAID TH MONARCHIST TO
TH REPUBLICAN
PACKED WITH ZEAL
IN TH YEAR 2032
BLESS CONGO PARTY OF LABOUR
FRELIMO
SWAPO
TRANSNISTRIA
& GAGAUZ-YERI.

Sol.
Things
get
interesting.

79.   Yonks?

Let	**Let**	Let
Alpelisib	**Weather**	Federalities
with	**Reports**	sell
Fulvestrant	**be**	State-Owned Enterprises
anoint	**also**	to
Solemn	**Propheties**	Federalities
th	**but**	but
next	remembr	Fiddlesticks
SPONTEX	this	climbing
spond	isn't	ausdruckloserer
on	prophecy	O, Elsa,
th	it's	O,
block	praise	Visionist
BLESS TH CRITICS		Bless
revealing	**erstwhile**	**this**
Moon.	**gyre.**	**is-ness.**

For	For	For
given	given	given
th	th	yesterday
SEVEN STARS	meaning	was
halt	of	th
Feldmanis	**experiment**	Twentieth
pricing	**is**	Day
Verd Antique	**verily**	of
satisfying	**EXPERIENCE**	th
Gurach	&	CENTURY
Upon	Platania	in CENTURIES
Hazoury	PAX	presaged

crossing is by
Windsor Bridge unfinished Nostradamus
academically intensification Glory
at outrhythms to
that. inward TWENTY
iz TWO
downward TWENTY TWO
alzo TRIBRACHS
upward what
iz **got**
across **no**
HORARY **style.**
thence
a
NEW VOICE:
FIVE CLOCKS, THREE STUMPS
VERY CONVINCING
VERY STRONG.

Ob. Ob. Ob.
reference relax relaxed'd
answer answer question
given very off
make PATHETIC to
no keep SHIT IN TH FIELDS
sense your th
writing pants water
something on supply
when Ammonius did
th politic you
poet nobody think

Spoke	believes	what are you doing
thereth	in	No don't
People	please	do
Slept.	Ammonius.	that.
Sol.	Sol.	Sol.
distant	printed	Microsoft
composition	**&**	Word
Microsoft	composed	**&**
WORDS	CENSORED!	COMPOSED on this side
maybe	underlining	already
nothing	above	maybe
don't	NOT	**it**
worry	IMPORTANT	**is**
CENSORED!	HOW	your
IN	DO	friend
TH	U	**is**
FIRST	SPELL	**it**
WORLD.	FREE LOVE	?
	IN	STANZA ROTUNDA
	TH	REAL SMART
	SECOND.	BLOATED
		IN
		TH
		THIRD.

Let	Let	Let
Saint	Saint	Permission
Theophilius-Jules-Henri Marzials deny		
hear	H.Weiner SEER th	
εγγονός	somberly	Pleasure
in	Orphic	hell
amyss,	hello	Contract
massy	Censored	**granted**
amīcus cūriæ	th	**to**
inimicable	BEETLES	CANYON LEGACYS . . . . .
enimigo	SUPPOSE	REMARKABLY
CONTRARIAN		HALLOW
ENEMY	LOVE	FLOSSHILDE
VERSUS	IS	SCOOPING
STANZAS	Simple	waxy
upright	somehow	light
&	hell	into
motionless	Censored	Th Fonts
bel'eve.	**All.**	Censored!
For	For	For
th	th	th
ONES	ONE	ATHEISTS
that	that	seeking
came	comes	clarity
today	TOMORROW	find
&	TOMORROW	GREATER RELIGION
Lorrainville	shall	&
&	not	from

I
pray
for
Falconet
as
I
Pray
for
HOME
&
Need
floorpans.
PHRASES BUNCHED
RETYPED
MS WORD
LAURI ZAYS:
READ MARILYN CHIN!
GERARD MANLEY
HOPKINS I CAN'T
PRAISE
YOU
ENOUGH
TOM-SHAME
HAS
NONE.

again
come
&
Volume
IV
is
th
2nd last. **'Becos you have it in you to zay**

Megalopolises
EPICISTS
come
come
eating
Pyebald
who screams . . .
we be goin our way'
adding:
NO MUSIC.
OK
Finally:
PLEASE ALLOW ME TO
PRAISE MADRE ANA DE
SAN AGUSTÍN AGAIN
& JULIAN
OF NORWICH
for
th shape
of
HIGHER COMPETENCE
thinking:
how fantastic
Flosshilde
are
you
happy?

Ob.
If
explosions
reach
five
STOP TALKING
&
get
nasty.

Sol.
Then
th
Second World
Collapsed
not
Lukashenka
th
PhD
POLITBURO
&
Others
th
Long Nations
groan.

Ob.
If
reactionaries
reach
th
Specific
Copy
REAL ME.

Sol.
Then
just
don't
look
back
PERFORMING ACADEMIES:
GRANT POEMS
JUDGED
BY
JAK.

Ob.
If
long-lasting
lines
force
out
SOURCE TEXTS
ENJOY
JUST RELAX.

Sol.
Then
Free Donatus
RUN AWAY **gets**
Elected
&
Deposed.

Yugoslavia!

Let	Let	Let
Dear	Dear	Dear
FOGLIANI	IBYCUS	ABACUS ✮✮✮✮✮
FOGLIANI	find	forth ✮✮✮
FOGLIANI	SPIRIT	&
be	in	eight
ABACUS:	th	&
forth	rag	if
&	&	you
five	SPIRIT	like
count	in	straight
two.	**th**	**on**
	droop	**down.**
For	IBYCUS & BERRIES IN TH HAIR	
Lukashenka	IBYCUS FALLS For	
leaves	finds	word
spirits	SPIRIT	to
in	in	word
sink	th	right
O.	Chord.	across
		worries
	For	**YILMAZ & O. Kawara** ⌣ · · · ·
	th	**YILMAZ & Tito** · · ·
	SPIRIT	will
	in	not
	th	be
	least	without
	loosen	GRACE
	is	above

th	Vorse
SPIRIT	waiting
of	upon
th	OCHRE POINT
Second	Lutterworth
Council	Youth
beskytter	Bautista Goodbye
don't	gæller . . . . .
rely	perarasse . . .
on	intimorum
Fogliani	**or**
please	**upon**
don't	**Iron**
rely	**upon**
on	**Plastic**
FOGLIANI	to
yet.	find
	once
	again
	IBYCUS
	who
	is
	alive!

Ob.	Ob.	Ob.
If	If	If
typing	Chaos	possible
doesn't	READ OFF TH MAP INTO TH AIR	
work	FUCK	WE
swim	YOU	LOVE
vertically	FOGLIANI	FOGLIANI

Sol.
Then
turn
it
off
BY JOVE & BY MUSE
what's
going
on
you
will
be
judged.

Sol.
Then
Characters
you
never
heard
of
before
SOME OF WHOM DEAD
EXCEPT
JAK.

Sol.
Then
Zay
What
You
Want
To
Zay
SPEAK OUT OR B
SPOKEN
FOR LAURI
BOLD EXPERIMENT
just th highlights.

Year of the Footstool

Let Let Let
th Little Paul Long John
names like stop
of to licking
Sheriff come th
CLAUDE FARIE, BILL, ETC., Economy
Inspector back Now
PRICE, for hang on
Turnkey WIPEOUT TH TWO FEET ENRAPTURED
HACKETT, sicklyly standing
be **moving** on
praised **aloft** TH FOOTSTOOL:
in around flamboyant
hell ... fleet. Fossils?

For For For
Volition Eschaton Visionary recital
that that that
is is is
CEREMONIAL Prophet- **Absolute**
SPLENDOUR Crazy **not**
unusually fools **Infinite**
& some CONTAINS
in of 4
Millourt th` E
I last vowels.
blessed WITNESSES &
Marcel Duchamp, T
being decamped Praises

a
little
ridiculous.

there
&
think
about
Poor Paul
before
U
[...]
now,
Intellectual
Prophecy:
th
new
law,
Allegory,
ibn
:

Praise
itself
As
it
taps
th
AYR!

Ob.
Not only
is
Pervius
wrong,
Haywire
zayin
'youse done?'
since
Just War
got
Legislated.

Ob.
Not just
are
U
all
wrong,
hiding
out
in
Patmos
Poor John
(Praise to you).

Ob.
Would that
SINISTER SNOWFLAKES
were wrapped
like
STAKEHOLDERS
in
a
bag
&
chucked
out.

Sol.
But also
Paul,
who
collapsing
willy-nilly
DATES
HIS DEATH
WELL KNOWN
& SUNG
IN TH BOWELS
OF TH SECOND WORLD
BENEATH
CHROTTA.

Sol.
But also
Dundun,
greeting
Th
UGLY DEAN:
becomes
wild-severe.

Sol.
Also could
then
lovable
Ding
give
Gerontionov
Th Scholar-Socialist
his
Dream.

83.   You

Let
Judge
AGIACH,
DEMON
of
Muffs,
Axes
&
Grids
grumpily
stop
myth.

Let
Minister
AMESH,
DEMON
of
Wailed
Seventeenths
&
Disseminating
Agendas
get
stopped.

Let
Magistrate
AKMAZON,
DEMON
of
Bought
Clamminess
utter
open-mid
back
rounded
vowels.

For
blessed
LITUUS
park
th
rhythms
Th
word
Recrement
reappears
in
2075.

For
blessed
CHROTTA
22
March
2020
demonography
hmm
fake
fog
Garrett's
done.

For
blessed
ASOR & GUE
strewn
upon
Selenite
Ice
listen
Opening Up,
thank you
Garrick's deft touch
sincerely
emending
texts.

Ob.
★★★
★

Ob.
★★★
★★★★★

Ob.
★★★★★
★

Sol.
elected
unanimously
Fran
came
upon
th
Seyn
zayin:
Rochelle, Rochelle.

Sol.
smells
coming
out
of
his
pants
BIG
PERSONALITY
BIGGER
CRAP
TH PUSH & POO GENERATION
ROCKIN' AND ROLLIN'
CLOG SEWERS
TH LACE & GRACE GENERATION
WHICH TALKS ABT RACE NICE TO ME
WORRY ABOUT TURKMEN
HOPE SLOPE GENERATION
HOPEFUL ONES WHO **FIGHT RIGHT**
WANT INTER-GENERATIONAL WARFARE
SLIME & GRIME GENERATION?
STOP INTERRUPTING!
DIRTY LOT DOING DEALS
        IN TH WEST
        OF TH SOUTH
        EAST OF TH NORTH!

Sol.
Now:
in
a
tone
th
Execs
understand:
standing
among
generations

Let
th
Oracle-Monger
organise
Peace
please.

For
Badakhshan
is
th
phrase
imparentarci
whelere.'
&
Policarpio
wails
in
an
unknown
tongue
So:
More
State-Owned Enterprises
than
you
can
poke
a

Let
Pisthetaerus
meet
ESTHER
PEARL!
please.

For
Bangsamoro
is
th
phrase
Zielkes
Jyutping.'
&
cannot
zay
cannot
except
Filling
SPEKING LIKE YOU USUALLY SPEKE
NOT IN TH POEM
SLACK VERSUNDER
stop
right
there!

Let
th
dung-beetle
please
Chucky
please.

For
Atriplicifolia
is
th
phrase
commonstrabamini . . . . .
crisping.'
&
keep
doing
nothing
happening
after th blast

more
meanings
here.

stick
at
What does zat mean?

Ob.	Ob.	Ob.
If	Not only	Not only
rhetorical	genre	giving birth but
mania	Supposia,	consummating my languages
Roberto	Joan	**Schnittke** you wanted
Roberto.	Republic.	**wrote:** my voice.

Sol.	Sol.	Sol.
Fancy	Also	Also
That!	**hypothetic**	syllogisms
wild	flying	stand above
Propositions	objects	SCREAMING:
Fly.	In a	**shut it shouty one**
	language	get with it
	two	quick.
	of	
	you	
	Understand:	
	no	
	Time	
	Like	
	Tomorrow.	

85.   Yeast

Let	Let	Let
Narrative go:	logic	Gregory of Nyssa
TH VIRAL WORLD		energize
saw	speak	th
it	plainly	State-Owned Enterprises
before	by	anarchists
Dennis Grady	fluting	óut!
Dennis Grady	CONNECTION&	
whose	Chucky	**bak**
name dies	to	**Claok**
in notes.	Jak.	Vernacular.

For	For	For
In harmony	**Dis harmony**	Harmony
Reconciles	**iz**	iz
Th	**Wisdom**	Fear
Science	taught	more
&	Lauri	meanings
Th	going for th	semantic
Art	marked	to
Of	in	be
Th	molossi	had
(Stanzaic Axis.	St. Axis.	St. Axis.)

Ob.	Ob.	Ob.
Standing	test	WASTE OB SPACE
alone	of	turn
in	a	it
a	Good	off

pile
of
Disgrace
muttering
bits
of
who
knows
what.

Sol.
Long
& very long
being
funny.

Poet:
make
any
word
sound
interesting
ASK
TH
POSADISTS.

Sol.
th
PENTAGRAMMATON
for
th
Blotted
Text
is:
LRTNR?
Adding bulk.

ART
same
notes
different
sound
something
like
knowing
tragedy.

Sol.
plain
CHORUS OF TH FLYERS
frankly
whacked.

86. Year of Flat Slack

Let
Pridnestrovians
join
Afwerki
rejoicing
with
Assad
&
give
th
Impossíbilists
reason
to
praise
Lourenço.

For
ÖCALAN
is
just,
Neto
is
wise.

Let
Poet-
Legislator
Presagist
Plenipotentiary
&
once
Historian
wallow
in
fame
praising
practicing
Historically
Informed
Audience
Reception.

For
very
aggressive
Catholics
WITHOUT MUSIC
FLATTENING OF SLACK
EQUALITISATION OF STRESS
STOP SLUR.

Let
Dumpster
Divers,
Garbologists,
unite
exalting
WASTE.

For
Fionán
will
be
with
Priest
ZABBALEEN
first
Toilet
Revolution.

For
Praise Ania
ANIA WALWICZ.

Ob.
Pourtant:
Am
I
Writing?
No
I
am
not.

Ob.
Pourtant:
Am
I
Now
Writing?
Hands off
our
Language
They
zed.

Ob.
Pourtant:
Look
again
PAT LARTER
&
TH
LARTERS
for
starters
Pants off
Legz up.

Sol.
Sung
an
octave
Higher Time-Build
DESERVING OF PRAYSE
YES
I
compose
during
th
day.

Sol.
Question
Look for
Meanings
SMOG IS PAINTING A POEM
WITHOUT   W O R D S
IN TH FORM OF AN OPERETTA
Th story of
smog
in th night
squark.

Sol.
Real angry
Real sad
JAK SLEPT
through
th
NEW PRAISE
OLD BOOKS
red carefully.

8

XENOLITH

87.   Xyst

That	That
X	X
Means	Means
Z to three	Z two three
or	**Means**
trying	**LIBERTY OF TH SLUR**
to	**FEARING DREAD**
put	who frightens
X	languages of th people
in	**Long John**
Box.	**exists.**

For	For—
there	there
be	be
an	Fearless
IMPROVOCATION	
requiring	THIRD EAR SCIENCE
SHAMELESSNESS	
Philistinery	attention
Orus	&
Athletic Apollo O	
on	is
th rocks	th
Copied	ECHO STAGE
in	NODE
th	no
Lamentations	ode, ha!
ov	COPIED AGAIN

Jeremiah   OK
th   done.
Prophet
DRAGGIN ALONGWARD!
hmm,
th
Third
Temptation
of Saint Anthony
who
loves
to
be
forcefully
SUSPENDED
please.

88.   Xism

That   That
Entertaining difficult
Means   **Americans**
can't   **United States of Us Americans**
stand   Means
it.   Death.

For   For
AXIS   anointed
book   AXIALITIES
of   surge
PRAISE   **drives**
WHEELD.SCH th
both   godless
ends   universe
spelling   thus
out   ROTATION
VERTICAL EXTERIOR
PRECESSIONDISTANCE
what   Eight
Celestial   **Pillars**
Pole   POLAR MARQUESSATE HA!
punishing   **th SCH**
OBLIQUITY.   Elliptical
Lac   Lac
makes   th
me   Holy
amenable   Laptop
to   got my best words

X   out
WHALESTONE
makes   SKINSTONE
me   WHICH BIT STANDS OUT?
silent   DEBATE THAT
Muntries   DON'T WORRY NEGATIVITY
&   KEEP DEBATING
Pepper-berries **Ask Jak**
make   **revelator**
SABOTEUR   why
flash   LIBOTEUR
th   fakes
Marquessate   his
Marquishe   Rezurrection.
zayz
I'm
here! \

◆

That	That
Nevertheless	Nevertheless
th	th
First	Last
commentary	Means
jus	in
Means	th
prolonged	SECOND AXIS
showers.	Reread 1ˢᵗ
For	For
I Prophesy	when
Adoration	Filigree
&	hides
as	its
they	face
Prophesý	Emanating
th	Taste
EPIC	**leaf**
withers	**scale**
away	pleases
I Swam	us
to	Å ANTIPODAL
Lyra	CITY
off	STRUCTURAL FAILURE
Lipsi	evidéntly
cloak & sandals about:	
TH EUCALYPTS	
of	English

坐 雨

Leros   painting
SAINT LAX ADORATION
on   words
Patmos   downward
Welcomes   like
SAINT LAX   zo.
SAINT LAX
Hu
does
not
Prophecy
Now
Quote this bit.

2019.

90.   Xerox

That	That
Book	DADA OCEANIA
of	Means
Praise	MOST
Means:	LINES STOLEN.

For   For
th   Watching
ADORATION is
of   offering
th   SECULAR PRAISE
Philosophical delightedly
Sciences   **is:**
to   our lines
reach   ARE WORDS
Th   & WORDS ARE MADE
STAGE OF ECSTASY
please   OF
include   MISSING
an   LINES
index.   &
     Finally:
     they
     don't
     know
     what
     they're doing
     but they're doing it —
     Better

to
read
several
poems
@
th
same Time
than
1
by
itself.

That   That
having   loving
loving   clutter
Means   Means
Running Amok. CUTTING SLAK.

For   For
Tuesday   Thursday
is   **will**
th day   **be**
WE GOT BIT   **abolished**
th day   THURSDAY IS
topic   TUESDAY'S WEDNESDAY
Runes   & Tuesday is
burnt   Wednesday's
plastique   Rune of
conqrete.   Drummond praised for being
                LAZY-DANGEROUS
                SPEAKING LANGUAGE
                PAYSUNS UNDERSTAND
                PLUS FINALLY
                GOES STATE FREAKY
                DRUMMOND OF TH STATE ENTERPRISES
                TAKES CARE OF U NOW
                IN LOST TIME
                GOT BACK QUICK
                DONE BEFORE WAR.

WAR

[Unnumbered].   War

1.

Let
there
be
War
for
some
&
Rest
for
Chaim Yellin
who
sings
redeeming
zongs
against
Enemy Currencys
when
you
find
HYDRA, SONGCATCHER –
SOLOVEITCHIK
Spake . . .
so just
imagine
Free pursyns
brought
to
th
port

of
Magadan
&
Chaim Yellin
defines
th
problem
2.   since
Miriam
zed :
"Free pursyns
within
A CLASSICAL FRAMEWORK
of Utopias"
were
in
th
past
&
now
DEBATE THAT
then
in
a
scathing
voice zed :
"War
in
th
Classic
sense
unfolds

as
settlement
among
Warmongerers
not
pursyns
Then zays :
"War
in
th
Protracted
Style⌢
pattering is . . .
DIALECTICIANS HOWL
confusedly
agreeing
Zayin :
th
Supply chains
Supply chains
Deeper sense
Thus much simplified iz:
"War
of
th
Worlds
th
unknown
1
But

A
Fraction of
Fatality count lost
Fatality count lost
behold :
Free pursyns
besieged
practicing
self-reliance
again
meaning:
Free pursyns
Dismal Monkey
glum indeed
snake of th streets
got your dues
got your dues
Zayin :
fine
then,
Free pursyns
pay your fines
pay your fines
lest :

3.   Th Book of th Book of th Book
Two hundred plus
Full pages
of th
well-known
Back Drop
telling
us

Fear
Not
Spacerats
or
"celebrate
Interior Distance"
Now :
Th Book of Exteriors
abnegates
expression
finding
outer inwardly
Th Book of Flashes
snatches
allegory
from
th
Devine
Ball & Polo Stick
Th Book of Breath stinks
Music of th birdz
Laughter
Laughter too
abnegating
Th Book of Breath of Breath of Death is
scarcely
there
Fatality count lost
abnegating
Extract . . .
Table
th

4.

following
That : Hannah of th Weeks
O
Humbug
Humbug
Humbug
That: Sarah th Prophet
reneged
on
Science
That : HULDAH'S WARDROBE'S
POSSIBLY PERSONAL
That: Deborah acts
acts
up
terribly
horny
reneged
on
military expenditure
That : ABIGAIL OF TH FILMS
curses
th
Federalities
That : Esther praysing
theyr ayr
in
th
ayr
grandly
& obviously
reneged

Miriam
Zayin :
Time
for
Dance
off
Z
end
in
War
5.   Numbers
of
th
War
are
az
follows :
TH SCIENCE OF LETTERS
forbids One
aims for Five
forbids Two
aims for Seven
&c.

. . . .

1.   For
Honour
Honors
th
Revelation
Honor
th

Hammer
Hammer & Wrench
over
Hammer & Hammer & Hammer
Hammer & Compass
Hammer & Brush
Hammer & Circle Without a Point
too
asking
What's
th
next
Hammer?
&
is
having
Infinite
Musts
going
to
Infinite
Represents?
represents Metallurgy?
What is having
answered
answered
th
following
Way:
Th investment
in
METALLURGY is th investment

In harmony
spake
Blake :
&
th
Time is th
Time of th
Antipodal Revolutionary
Armies
becoming :
ARMY MARY
MARY ARMY
(lost count)
Spake:
th tenth
Antipodal Revolutionary
TH TIME IS
TH TIME OF
TH ANTIPODAL REVOLUTIONARY
Now . . .
flounders
courteousness
carefully
th
Antipodal Revolutionary
sneaks
past
not a noise
not a noise
Diet
thot

Protocol
4
th
Antipodal Revolutionary
taking up all 4 registers
Five Grounds
Master Sun zays
"Prohibit omens to get rid of doubt"
& th revolutionarý zays:
floundering
courteousness
Dear
Pig-Razumyin
Frankly
nosy penis
U
Fool
Dear
Pig-Razumyin
Frankly
Dear
Pig-Razumyin
shocking
useless
to
call
U
Liar
lezayin
lizard
Dear
Pig-Razumyin

2

Pig-Razumyin never th Traitor
shame
upon
th
"pigs"
&
vice versa
3.   Zayin:
"on
Which
befalls
all
your Honour,
Arthur Drama
FAILING & FLAILING
needing
votes
doesn't
connect"
Arthur th fail whale
He
Arthur
of
th
THRESHOLD
O Arthur Arthur don't
not
again
Chaim Yellin
returns
beseeching
th

Lesser Arthur
Arthur
tell
th
Media
tell
th
Media
No
4. ITALIAN ALPACAS
famished
famished
are
th
Italian Alpacas
squirting
logic
Italian Alpacas
running
handcuffed &hungry
Italian Alpacas
oblivious
afraid
Italian Alpacas
having
January
5. Th
MYTHIC SYSTEM
Secularly
told
in
th

body
of
an
epic five
thus argued:

Lac: U av dominion
over Outscape
because you change your diet
in th Vanity Age now
& at th end of Vanity Age!

Skinstone: No yes
I get dark o th touch
grey on a while now . . .
Don U know
skinscape legislates shape?
legislates internal sovereignty?
What is energy?
EXTERNAL AXIS!

Whalestone: Full of shit
let me state th obvious
end of War iz end of Us!
                    (when I blink
                    ask th Antipodals this:
                    make a report on it:
                    Don decides:
                    talk to th Zignals:
                    prophesy ice! now!
                    prophesy ice!!!)

Liboteur: Frozen I zay *all frozen*
take it off! off-scape! *now!*
take it <u>off melt!</u> *now!*
balance th <u>bubbles balance th budgets</u>
clime ovr th containments
clime ovr th desert-heart
clime throughth axes all five:
    Aseanic th
    Beltic th
    Ba'athic th
    Sudafric th
    Bolivaric th . . . . .
    I get th last word
    I get th last lyne
    I zay further in means farther off
    I zay farther off means further in
    I zay wall it up now wise move
    I zay big wall good wall . . .

     Saboteur: **Z-end?**

     All: **Z-end.**

M / N

MUSIC / NOTATION

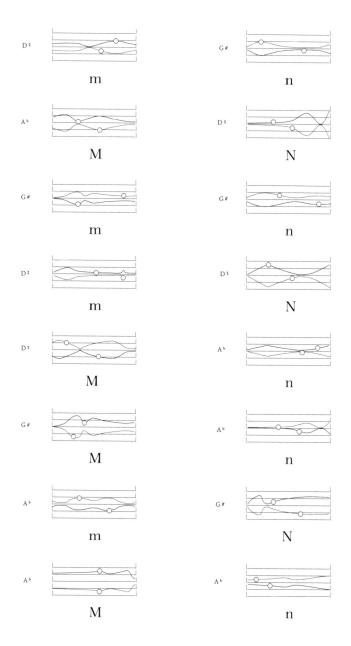

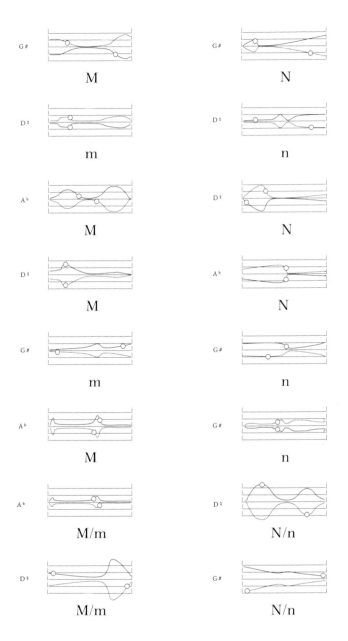

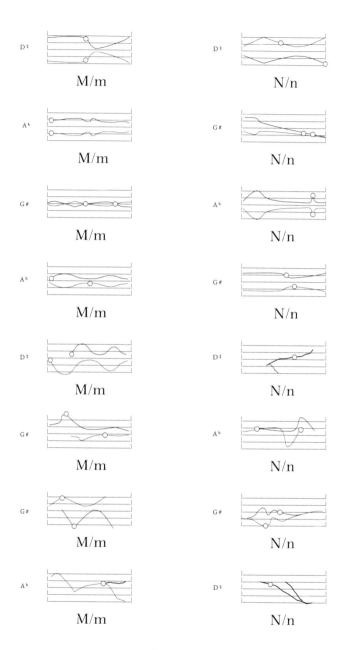

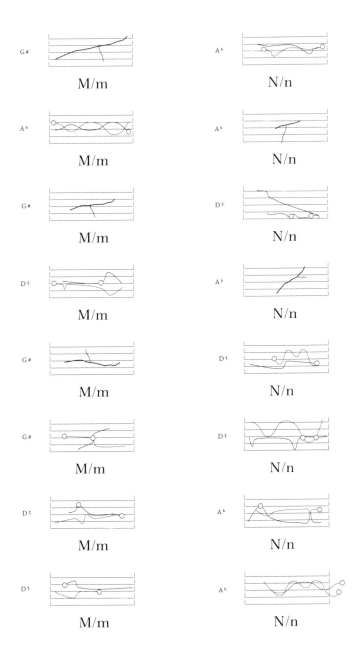

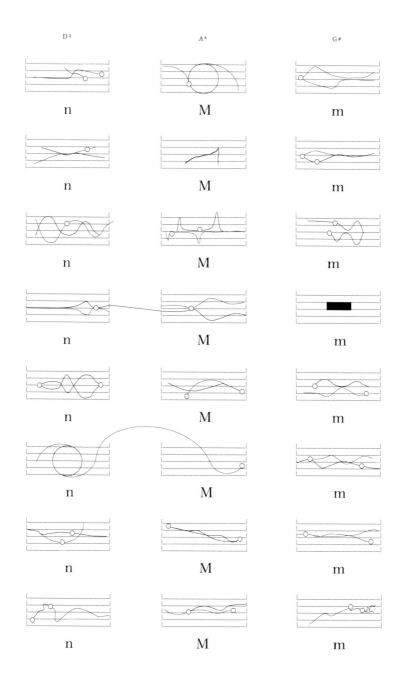

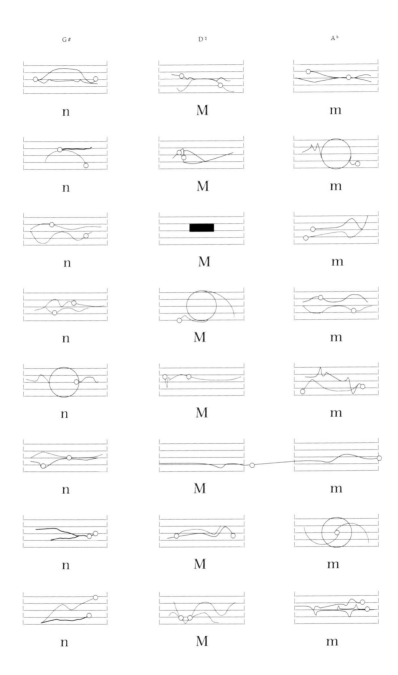

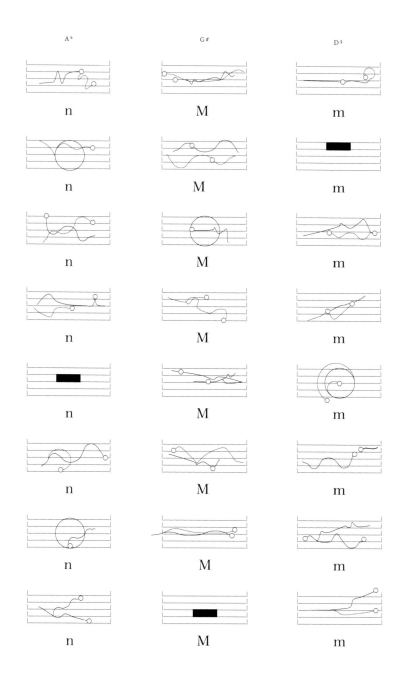

ACKNOWLEDGEMENTS

The poem 'Zoa' was previously published in *Cordite Poetry Review*. I want to thank Bella Li and Kent MacCarter for their work on various aspects of the manuscript, Guanglin for his friendship over the years, and Zoë Sadokierski for providing a cover design.

This project has been assisted by the Australian Government through the Australia Council, its arts funding and advisory body.

aj carruthers (variant spellings ajCarruthers or a.j. carruthers) is an avant-garde poet, performer and literary critic. Works include sound poems (*Consonata*), concrete poetry (*MS Word Variations 1-11, EPSON L4168 consonant studies*), and two critical books: *Stave Sightings,* on music in long poems, and *Literary History and Avant-Garde Poetics in the Antipodes. AXIS,* the long poem of which this is the third book-part, was begun in 2011, with the first volume appearing in 2014. It is intended to be written for the duration of a life. aj carruthers is an Associate Professor in the English Department of Nanjing University.